# WADING IN WAIST-HIGH WATER

Published by Tin House, Portland, Oregon

Distributed by W. W. Norton & Company

Library of Congress Cataloging-in-Publication Data

Names: Pecknold, Robin, author. | Taylor, Brandon (Brandon L. G.) writer of
    introduction.
Title: Wading in waist-high water : the lyrics of Fleet Foxes /
    introduction by Brandon Taylor ; songs, notes, and afterword by Robin
    Pecknold.
Description: Portland, Oregon : Tin House, 2022.
Identifiers: LCCN 2022024983 | ISBN 9781953534446 (hardcover) | ISBN
    9781953534521 (ebook)
Subjects: LCSH: Songs--Texts. | Fleet Foxes (Musical group) | LCGFT:
    Popular music lyrics.
Classification: LCC ML54.6.P413 W33 2022 | DDC
    782.42164026/8--dc23/eng/20220525
LC record available at https://lccn.loc.gov/2022024983


Printed in the USA
Interior design by Jakob Vala

www.tinhouse.com

# WADING IN WAIST-HIGH WATER

## The Lyrics of Fleet Foxes

Introduction by Brandon Taylor

Songs, Notes, and Afterword by Robin Pecknold

TIN HOUSE / Portland, Oregon

# CONTENTS

# INTRODUCTION
Brandon Taylor

When laid out on the page in stark black ink, the songs of Fleet Foxes have the look and feel of mid-century American poems: direct, conversational, and flecked with an emotional urgency verging on the surreal. There is an inwardness to the songs, but also an awareness of others, an almost-fear of navel-gazing or self-indulgence. The speakers of these songs are wary of putting on or being perceived as putting on. Like their stylistic forebears—Dylan, Cohen, Young—Robin Pecknold's lyrics are suffused with a longing to return to a long-vanished and perhaps entirely fictional pastoral way of life: nature and its many facets, both beautiful and dangerous, rise to the level of a unifying character in these songs. These are folk songs, after all.

Or, I suppose, they are contemporary songs in the spirit of American folk music with all of its Whitmanic impulses. But in the hands of Fleet Foxes, the pastoral feels less like a particular zone in time and more like a space in which to parse ideas of self-reliance, the inconstancy of love, the pain of intimacy, the fear of loss, the sting of betrayal, and the strange but urgent project of hope. For instance, the early song "Sun Giant," from the EP of the same name, has the form and structure of a traditional folk work song, right down to the theme of praising the blessing of good weather and the virtues of being alive: "What a life I lead in the summer / What a life I lead in the spring" and "What a life I lead when the sun breaks free / As a giant torn from the clouds" and the beautiful repetition of "What a life" at the end of the second verse.

This repetition feels at first like rejoicing and then, in the revisiting, or perhaps in the greater context of the Fleet Foxes lyrical oeuvre, the repetition harbors something of a lamentation. Because in a Fleet Foxes song, life isn't just life. You can't simply enjoy it. There is always, lingering at the edges, the realization that time is passing, inevitably, onward and out of your hands. That every life is lost. Every moment goes on without you. Consider these lines from "Drops in the River," also from the *Sun Giant* EP: "Crown of leaves, high in the window on a gold morning / Young today, old as a railroad tomorrow / Days are just drops in the river to be lost always." The transience of time and the ephemeral nature of our relationships are two of the great themes of these songs. I started to think of it as a Pecknoldian paradox: things change, they always change; even memory is transient. Human relationships last only in our telling of them, and memory is what grants meaning to our relationships. Memory is all that we have amid the inconstancy of the human heart. And eventually that too will fail us when we need it most—we are alone.

So many Fleet Foxes songs hinge on the speaker's realization, imagined or otherwise, that they are alone and the past is a place to which they can never repatriate. Consider these lyrics from "Innocent Son": "Rustling leaves falling beside me / On a ghost of a morning / Riding in sorrow to the harbor / Far behind, o' me, / The bodies of my friends / Hanging alone, alone again" and from "Sim Sala Bim," which ends with "Remember when you had me cut your hair? / Call me Delilah then / I wouldn't care." In "Isles," the speaker professes, "And I don't even miss you at all / No, no."

While the key of this realization of the past's ever-receding horizon is often that of lament and sorrow, the songs take on a different relationship to the past starting with the album *Crack-Up* and continuing with *Shore*. In "Third of May / Ōdaigahara," the speaker says, "Light ended the night, but the song remained / And I was hiding by the stair, half here, half there / Past the lashing rain / And as the sky turned petal white, old innocent lies came to mind / As we stood, congregated, at the firing line." While frankness and honesty have always been hallmarks of the speakers of Fleet Foxes songs, that frankness and honesty have often been self-excoriating and punitive. That is, self-revelation through the first few albums came with the heat of self-mutilation. But here, a mature backward gaze blends an awareness of the speaker's own role in things going horribly wrong with a kind of openheartedness, seen in lines like "Oh, but I can hear you, loud in the center / Aren't we made to be crowded together like leaves?" and "Was I too slow? / Did I change overnight?" We see it again in "If You Need To, Keep Time on Me," in the lyrics "How could it all fall in one day? / Were we too sure of the sun?" It's the *we* that feels important there because it implies shared culpability in the downfall of the subject being mourned. And, from *Shore*, songs like "Young Man's Game" and "Featherweight" are playful in their rueful reflections on past pretensions and the cost of masculine gesture and posturing. The nostalgia is less distorting and less brutal in the later albums, and as such, it feels more like wisdom.

Also central to Fleet Foxes songs are the Pecknoldian pairs—brothers, friends, lovers, and shadow selves. Songs like "Mykonos," "Blue Ridge Mountains," "Your Protector," "Tiger Mountain Peasant Song," "The Shrine / An Argument," "Can I Believe You," "Fool's Errand," and "Innocent Son" all converge on relationships. In a Fleet Foxes song, there is the one who loves and the one who betrays. The one who flees and the one who is abandoned. Regret. Loss. The fear of committing. Sometimes the other half of a Pecknoldian dyad isn't even another person, but a different version of the speaker themselves. In the early songs, this often takes the form of a self-interrogation or murder. A body lost. An argument resulting in severed communication. In the later songs, the dyad is more abstract, a relationship between the speaker and themselves, and the lyrics take on a more rhetorical resonance. In "Can I Believe You," on 2020's *Shore*, the speaker asks, "Can I believe you when you say I'm good / I didn't need to when I wished you would / No it isn't enough," and "Can I believe you? / I want to need you." It's hard to imagine a speaker of a Fleet Foxes song ever saying that on the earlier records, when self-revelation always came with such a painful, extractive cost.

While these songs have a Jungian force to them, they are also steadfastly narrative. Rooted in a raconteur storytelling tradition, songs like "Third of May / Ōdaigahara," "I Should See Memphis, "Maestranza," "Mykonos," "White Winter Hymnal," and "Tiger Mountain Peasant Song" tell intricate stories that weave together the personal with the social and the historical. These songs hum with references to paintings, songs, books, and other art. There is something Chaucerian about them. The speakers are not merely delivering abstract notions of life; they move among particular forests at particular times of the day and year. We feel the snowmelt under our feet. The tinkle of ice in the air. Or the salt spray of the ocean. Particularly in *Shore*, where so much of the album's mood hinges on evocations of "warm American water" and "some lost coast / some bright days." While the pre-*Crack-Up* songs certainly were more narrative in the mode of Dylan—bruisers, cruisers, and bloody knuckles, people moving through the shadowy edges of society, getting their hearts and hands broke—the narrative character of Fleet Foxes songs remains strong in *Shore*, though of a looser nature.

As an album, *Shore* feels somehow more novel-like, whereas the other albums feel more akin to short story collections or sets of vivid vignettes. In *Shore*, the tone is more reflective, continuous. The *I* in the "Wading in Waist-High Water" lyric "Soon as I knew you / All so wide open / Wading inside of fire / As if I just saw you," feels like the same *I* in the "Shore" lyric, "Kin of my kin, I rely on you / Taking me in, when a wave runs me through." Here is a consciousness moving through a particular period of contemplation, reaching a place of earnest, reflective vulnerability. Though the individual songs might be less explicitly narrative, the album overall is among the most narrative and cohesive of all Fleet Foxes albums. The story is broader, big picture. It unfolds across the whole body of the album.

There is something quite moving about seeing these fifty-five songs collected and assembled this way. Themes of family, friendship, love, destiny, loss, nature, and honest living bridge all of the albums and form the core set of concerns of this body of work. At the same time, you can see the evolution of the minds and hearts at work behind the lyrics. Fleet Foxes songs have always been that magic mix of vulnerable and tough, and there is something about the later songs, a certain opening up, that makes that vulnerability almost unbearably tender. That's one of the magic things about a volume like this. When you see it laid out in front of you, all those connections come into view. The changes, too. The way the lyric intelligence grows and shifts and becomes aware of its place in the world—it takes on new ambitious forms and projects for itself, consuming history and the personal in equal measure. It's a thrill, too, to realize that it's a still-evolving and growing body of work.

There is more to say, of course. There is always more to say about the songs that mean the most to us. After all, those songs are often what gives meaning to those moments, great and small, in a life when things change or begin to change. The songs that mean the most to us become a part of our own personal histories, and we turn to them to share bits of ourselves with others. Likewise, those songs return us to who we were at those particular moments in time. It's hard to give an accounting of a body of songs that means something to you without sharing some of yourself. These songs were my companions through moments of personal upheaval. They were the bedrock of my last major relationship, our way of speaking to each other. So many of these songs recall mornings I shared with an ex, making coffee and watching the sun come up or watching the fall over Lake Mendota in Madison. And, too, the winter I decided to blow up my life and pursue art. When I listen to *Crack-Up* or *Helplessness Blues*, it's always that summer when everything changed and deepened, and I made choices about who I wanted to be.

But I think in the end, what matters is that these songs are alive. They change in the way that great art changes—with your shifting perception and experience. The songs seem to shiver and breathe. They reward the living you gotta do to stay alive. You never quite come to a Fleet Foxes song and find the same thing, and isn't that truly the best kind of companion to take with you in life? One who is there, but never exactly the same. One who can show you who you are in different ways at different moments. This is another of their great themes: we are never as we once were, and we have to go on living anyway.

11/1/2021

# WADING IN
# WAIST-HIGH
# WATER

# FLEET FOXES
## JUNE 3, 2008

· SUN GIANT · DROPS IN THE RIVER · ENGLISH HOUSE ·
· MYKONOS · INNOCENT SON · ISLES · SUN IT RISES ·
· WHITE WINTER HYMNAL · RAGGED WOOD ·
· TIGER MOUNTAIN PEASANT SONG · QUIET HOUSES ·
· HE DOESN'T KNOW WHY · YOUR PROTECTOR ·
· MEADOWLARKS · BLUE RIDGE MOUNTAINS · OLIVER JAMES ·

# SUN GIANT

FLEET FOXES / 02:06

# SUN GIANT[1]

What a life I lead in the summer[2]
What a life I lead in the spring
What a life I lead when the wind it breathes
What a life I lead in the spring

What a life I lead when the sun breaks free
As a giant torn from the clouds
What a life indeed when that ancient seed
Is a-buried, watered and plowed
What a life[3]
What a life
What a life
What a life

---

*Is there room in the Seattle music scene for a cappella harmony?*

1. The first Fleet Foxes song—not actually, but spiritually.

2. After growing up in Seattle, living and working under the long shadow of grunge, it felt subtly subversive (at the time) to open a discography, and every early concert, with a quiet, sweet, a cappella moment. I remember early shows at megafestivals where we were tasked to go onstage after some deafeningly loud mainstream band; I'd watch and wonder if opening with "Sun Giant" right after would summon a pin-drop silence, or be completely lost in the tumult of the surrounding stages.

3. I feel that I should avoid mentioning hiking too much in these notes.

What a life I lead in the summer

What a life I lead in the spring

What a life I lead when the wind it breathes

What a life I lead in the spring[4]

---

# DROPS IN THE RIVER
## FLEET FOXES / 04:11

# DROPS IN THE RIVER[1]

Crown of leaves, high in the window on a gold morning[2]
Young today, old as a railroad[3] tomorrow
Days are just drops in the river to be lost always
Only you, only you, you know

Years ago, birds of a feather would arrive nightly
Gone you know, held to another like clutched ivy
On the shore, speak to the ocean and receive silence[4]
Only you, only you, you know[5]

---

*Can I write a rock song on a dulcimer?*

1. From a Jorge Luis Borges poem.

2. Recorded at Bear Creek Studios in Woodinville, Washington, with the legendary Phil Ek, who produced all my favorite albums as a teenager. My dad, Greg Pecknold, played bass, a bass he made himself, on one of the first albums made at Bear Creek, Linda Waterfall's *Bananaland*. Love you, Dad.

3. First and only occurrence of the word "railroad" in this catalog, let it be noted.

4. This image recurs in the album *Shore* and the first moments of its accompanying film.

5. This is one of those lyrics that grew out of the phonemic dictates of a vocalese-first songwriting process.

Here as the caves of my memory fade, I'll hold to the first one
I wouldn't turn to another you say, on the long night we've made
Let it go

Only you, only you, you know
Only you, only you, you know[6]

Here as the caves of my memory fade, I'll hold to the first one
I wouldn't turn to another you say, on the long night we've made
Let it go

Speak to me slow, my dear
No ghost, of course, in here
Pleased to be lonesome, quiet and clear
All is alone in here

---

6. Here's an example of a lyric where the phonemes used are completely dependent on and informed by the melody being sung. Lyrics can be hard to read on the page with the sung context missing, but thanks for humoring me.

# ENGLISH HOUSE
## FLEET FOXES / 04:40

# ENGLISH HOUSE[1]

You go with your two feet bare
Down through the cold lane there, to Brighton[2]
A country house, a liar and a louse live there
And go with your arms held wide
Happiness in your eyes, convincing
And stay the night, turn out every light you see
And lay them down, buried in the ground for me

---

*Can we blend Motown and freak folk?*

1. The *Sun Giant* EP was actually recorded after we finished the first Fleet Foxes album. We were heading out on our first national tour, and we needed something for the merch table, as the album wouldn't come out for another six months. Despite this, the EP is my favorite early document, and I think it really benefited from being made in a less pressurized context, with a whole musical vocabulary already well developed and a bright future ahead.

2. Like "railroad" in "Drops in the River," here's an example of a word that by its very presence came to define an aspect of the band's early identity. I remember going to England and being asked repeatedly about this reference to Brighton, and I remember being asked in American interviews about the band's inherent Englishness. Choose your words wisely, young bands!

My love
My love
My love
My love

The tongues of the creatures wag
Drawn to the fragile legs you walk on
A cold wind blows, Brighton to the coast for me
A cold wind blows, Brighton to the coast for me

My love
My love
My love
My love[3]

---

3. At thirty-six, I try to write songs that genuinely mean something, but when writing this at twenty-two, I can't say that was always true.

# MYKONOS
FLEET FOXES / 03:39

# MYKONOS[1]

The door slammed loud[2] and rose up a cloud of dust on us
Footsteps followed down through the hollow sound torn up

And you will go to Mykonos[3]
With a vision of a gentle coast
And a sun to maybe dissipate
Shadows of the mess you made

---

*Can I write a song with two choruses?*

1. This song survived many ill-considered early versions. We tried solo acoustic, neo-soul, heartland rock, and Pacific Northwest indie versions before landing on this arcane rock version. Still the most popular Fleet Foxes song, never topping it, thankful to it. I wrote it at 3:00 AM alone in our old practice space on Western Avenue in downtown Seattle, and walked home as the sun rose, conspiratorial, like I was the only person in the world who knew this great song now existed.

2. I sometimes like starting a song in medias res like this, right in the middle of descriptive action.

3. When I wrote this song, I was not at all aware that the island of Mykonos is a modern-day Greek mecca for parties and nightlife. I came across the word in an atlas somewhere and thought it fit the obliquely arcane sonic mood of the *Sun Giant* EP. I'm still waiting for the sync-request call from the Greek tourism council.

Pallid animals and the snow-tipped pines I find
Hatching from the seed of your orphaned mind all night

And you will go to Mykonos
With a vision of a gentle coast
And a sun to maybe dissipate
Shadows of the mess you made

Brother you don't need to turn me away
I was waiting down at the ancient gate

You go wherever you go today
You go today

I remember how they took you down
As the winter turned the meadow brown

You go wherever you go today
You go today

When out walking brother, don't you forget
It ain't often that you'll ever find a friend

You go wherever you go today
You go today

# INNOCENT SON

## FLEET FOXES / 03:06

# INNOCENT SON[1]

You left me there,
Waiting at the bottom of the stairs with my eyes closed
Holding my right hand in my left
There is no time for hesitation now
You come or go, or go[2]

Rustling leaves falling beside me
On a ghost of a morning
Riding in sorrow to the harbor
Far behind, o' me,

---

*Can I make a song that would belong on* If I Could Only Remember My Name *by David Crosby?*

1. The narrator of these songs doesn't seem to feel much agency. Lots of waiting, being abandoned, and watching things happen.

2. I wrote all these early songs at ages twenty and twenty-one while living in a pre-gentrification, $400-a-month studio apartment on Seattle's Capitol Hill. It was as close as I've come in my life to some bohemian ideal, seeing shows every night, interfacing with other musicians, playing in bands and exploring our city with wide eyes. I remember writing this song during an afternoon one summer and walking over to the old Chop Suey that night to play it for the first time, feeling like life was perfect and could never change.

The bodies of my friends
Hanging alone, alone again

Some twisted thorn
Tells me you saw me in the night with another
Keep all my promises to break them
I am no, o' no, innocent son

You run,
Rabbit
run³

---

3. John Updike.

# ISLES

FLEET FOXES / 03:06

# ISLES[1]

Everyone stares when you walk in the room
They stare when you go
You've got so much control
How could anyone say no?
They rarely do,
That's why you're you and why you're winning

And I don't even miss you at all[2]
No, no

Caught in the light, you would idly spin
Your skeleton ring
See it shine when you sing
To the window with no meaning
From Tennessee your harmony
Would leave your spirit

---

*Can I use a Joni Mitchell guitar tuning but make a song that doesn't sound like her?*

1. Recorded at Casey Wescott's old house in Burien, Washington, where we recorded many overdubs for the first Fleet Foxes album. This was a track that didn't fit anywhere except on the B side of a single in the UK, but it's one of my favorite early melodies.

2. Unconvincing.

And I don't even miss you at all
No, no

Silver the shores of isles up north
Boulevards of dancing boats

You keep the old ember burning
With meadows in mind
As the coaches go by
These thoughts of you will die
They rarely do
That's why you're you
And why you're winning

And I don't even miss you at all
No, no

Silver the shores of isles up north
Boulevards of dancing boats

Silver the shores of isles up north

# SUN IT RISES

FLEET FOXES / 03:14

# SUN IT RISES

Red squirrel in the morning
Red squirrel in the evening
Red squirrel in the morning[1]
I'm coming to take you home[2]

Sun rising over my head
In the morning when I rise
Hold me dear into the night
Sun it will rise soon enough

---

*Can we make a song that feels like the Beach Boys went to Ireland?*

1. Trigger warning: Squirrels, post-hoc justification. In the middle of making the first Fleet Foxes album, my siblings and I went on a family heritage trip to the UK and Norway to meet some distant relatives and see where our great-grandparents emigrated from. We were hiking in the Lake District, and kept seeing signs on the trails about the decimation of the native red squirrel population, a species that has been overtaken by the North American eastern gray squirrel. So we'd sing the dumb little song that opens the first album as we walked. If I wanted to make a huge intellectual leap, I could say that the first Fleet Foxes album is an example of an American band "coming for" a set of English influences and overtaking them, in the same way the gray squirrel overtook the red. More likely, though, I was just twenty-two years old, having fun making songs, and not thinking I'd be writing justificatory footnotes for them over a decade later.

2. First appearance of the word "home." More on this later.

Sun rising, dangling there
Golden and fair, in the sky[3]

---

3. So much of the natural imagery in these early songs grew out of a desire to simply translate the beauty we were trying to achieve in the musical arrangements into plain English, without narrative or emotion getting in the way.

# WHITE
# WINTER HYMNAL
FLEET FOXES / 02:27

# WHITE WINTER HYMNAL[1]

I was following the, I was following the
I was following the, I was following the
I was following the, I was following the
I was following the, I was following the

I was following the pack, all swallowed in their coats
With scarves[2] of red tied round their throats
To keep[3] their little heads
From falling in the snow[4]
And I turned round and there you'd go[5]

---

*Can we make a pop song that's mostly a cappella?*

1. This is now an accidental Christmas carol performed by middle school choirs internationally. Life is weird!

2. First and only appearance in the catalog of the word "scarves."

3. Are the scarves keeping their heads attached to their bodies somehow? Are these children somehow Frankensteined? Why am I following them?

4. Just the appearance of the word "snow" is enough to cement a song as a Christmas carol, apparently.

5. Where is he going?

And, Michael,[6] you would fall[7]
And turn the white snow red[8] as
Strawberries
In the summertime

---

6. I still get a lot of messages from people asking who Michael is. I don't know who Michael is.

7. Why did Michael fall?

8. Sometimes people send me clips of children's choirs covering this song, and it absolutely warms my heart every time. But if I read the comments, there will be at least one along the lines of "How can you make these kids sing this song, it's literally about decapitation??" To any choir directors reading this: Thanks for including "White Winter Hymnal" in your songbook. It's not about decapitation.

# RAGGED WOOD
FLEET FOXES / 05:07

# RAGGED WOOD[1]

Come down from the mountain[2]
You have been gone too long
The spring is upon us, follow my honest song
Settle down with me by the fire of my yearning
You should come back home,[3] back on your own now

---

*Can we write another song with two choruses?*

1. This song opens with a variant of what came to be known in think pieces as the "millennial whoop." Epidemiologists believe patient zero of the millennial whoop to be the song "Wake Up" by Canadian band Arcade Fire. The whoop spread from there and became endemic in the culture for a few years before the vaccine was eventually found. That said, this song still gets people dancing at shows and is very fun to play. The culture is currently experiencing an outbreak of Max Weinberg–influenced drum patterns, for which there is no known cure. Too catchy.

2. First appearance of only a few in the catalog of the word "mountain."

3. "Homes" two through five are in this song. I don't think "home" was really in the vocabulary of pop music at the time we writing this, and I'm not saying that this song or album are the reason that the word "home" became ubiquitous in the music you'd hear whenever you went to Walgreens in the decade after it came out. But on the off chance that that was our fault, I deeply apologize.

The world is alive now, in and outside our home
You run through the forest, settled before us, oh
Darling, I can barely remember you beside me
You should come back home, back on your own now
You should come back home, back on your own now

Evening light, when the woman of the woods came by
To give to you the word of the old man
Morning tide, when the sparrow and the seagull fly
And Jonathan and Evelyn[4] get tired

Lie to me if you will
At the top of Barringer Hill[5]
Tell me anything you want
Any old lie will do
Call me back to, back to you

Lie to me if you will
At the top of Barringer Hill
Tell me anything you want
Any old lie will do
Call me back to, back to you

---

4. People sometimes ask me, "Who are Jonathan and Evelyn?" I don't know who
Jonathan and Evelyn are. Probably friends of Michael's.

5. Not a real place.

# TIGER MOUNTAIN PEASANT SONG

FLEET FOXES / 03:28

# TIGER MOUNTAIN PEASANT SONG[1]

Wanderers this morning came by
Where do they go, graceful in the morning light?
To Banner Fair, to follow you softly
In the cold mountain air

Through the forest, down to your grave
Where the birds wait, and the tall grasses wave
They do not know you anymore

Dear shadow alive and well
How can the body die?
You tell me everything,
Anything true

---

*Can I write a song that feels like Judee Sill could have been involved?*

1. Tiger Mountain is a favorite hiking spot on the Eastside of Seattle. It is much less mystical than the tone of this song might suggest, though.

Into town one morning I went
Staggering through premonitions of my death
I don't see
Anybody that dear to me

Dear shadow alive and well
How can the body die?
You tell me everything,
Anything true

Jesy[2]
I don't know what I have done
I'm turning myself to a demon
I don't know what I have done
I'm turning myself to a demon

---

2. Written for a dear friend who showed me sides to the Pacific Northwest I never knew were there.

# QUIET HOUSES
## FLEET FOXES / 03:32

# QUIET HOUSES

Lay me down, lay me down[1]
Lay me down, lay me down
Darkening, darkening[2]
Darkening, darkening

Come to me, come to me
Come to me, come to me
Lay me down, lay me down
Lay me down, lay me down

---

*Can we blend Motown, barbershop, and Nintendo music?*

1. I have to be honest here: these lyrics are quite tertiary to the intended appeal of this song. Lyrics have come to mean a lot to me as a musician, and have always meant a lot to me as a listener, but I've never identified as a writer or had literary ambitions. I love building songs, building sonic worlds, finding an alchemy between notes and words and delivery and timbre that feels complete and transportive. Words are almost always an aspect to that, sometimes the primary aspect, but sometimes not. In this song they definitely were not! And yet it's one of my favorites on the album, musically.

2. People often ask what I'm saying here, if it's "darkening" or "donkey man." I don't know who the donkey man is, or why I'd be singing about him, but if you're reading this, donkey man, I just want to say I hope you're doing well, and I'm sorry if you thought this song was written for you when it wasn't.

Quiet houses, lit up by candlelight
In the gloom of the dawn
Quiet houses, lit up by candlelight
Light of an English song

# HE DOESN'T
# KNOW WHY
FLEET FOXES / 03:20

# HE DOESN'T KNOW WHY[1]

Penniless and tired with your hair grown long
I was looking at you there and your face looked wrong
Memory is a fickle siren's song
I didn't understand
In the gentle light as the morning nears
You don't say a single word of the last two years
Where you were or when you reach the frontier
I didn't understand

See your rugged hands and a silver knife
Twenty dollars in your hand that you hold so tight
All the evidence of your vagrant life
My brother, you were gone
And you will try to do what you did before

---

*Can an unused demo serve as a cast-off outro?*

1. With songs like "White Winter Hymnal" and this one, I remember trying to offset the joyful, rollicking nature of the music with some tale of loss or disappointment. I remember just repeating "penniless and tired" over and over again, and the rest of the lyric flowed from there.

Pull the wool over your eyes for a week or more
Let your family take you back to your
Original mind

There's nothing I can do
There's nothing I can do
There's nothing I can say
There's nothing I can say
I can say[2]

---

2. Musically, we were trying to land somewhere between the Band, the Beach Boys, and Nintendo music.

# YOUR PROTECTOR

## FLEET FOXES / 04:09

# YOUR PROTECTOR[1]

She left a week to roam
Your protector is coming home
Keep your secrets with you, girl
Safe from the outside world
You walk along the stream
Your head caught in a waking dream
Your protector's coming home, coming home

As you lay to die beside me, baby
On the morning that you came
Would you wait for me?
The other one would wait for me
As you lay to die beside me, baby

---

*What would a gothic rock song in a minor key sound like?*

1. I wrote this song after taking a trip with my siblings to Ireland, Norway, Scotland, and England, visiting local pubs and sitting in on *seisiúns*, marveling at the technicality and soul put into that traditional music. The debut album was quite stuck at this point—"White Winter Hymnal" seemed to point a clear way forward for the rest of it, but I still needed to write a few important songs and they just weren't coming. That trip, and falling in love with the music of Fairport Convention, Sandy Denny, and Pearls Before Swine helped guide the remainder of the writing.

On the morning that you came
Would you wait for me?
The other one would wait for me

You run with the devil
You run with the devil

Tell your brother to be good
Tell your sister not to go
Tell your mother not to wait
Tell your father I was good

As you lay to die beside me, baby
On the morning that you came
Would you wait for me?
The other one would wait for me

# MEADOWLARKS

FLEET FOXES / 03:11

# MEADOWLARKS[1]

Meadowlark, fly your way down
I hold a cornucopia and a golden crown
For you to wear upon your fleecèd down
My meadowlark, sing to me

Hummingbird, just let me die
Inside the broken ovals of your olive eyes
I do believe you gave it your best try
My hummingbird, sing to me

My hummingbird, sing to me

---

*Can we find a song on this broken pump organ from Goodwill?*

1. The speaker of this song is either some elfin lord of the forest or a guy shopping at a Michaels arts and crafts store.

Don't believe a word that I haven't heard
Little children laughing at the boys and girls
The meadowlark singing to you each and every night
The arc light on the hillside and the market in the hay[2]

---

2. These two songs in a row here, "Your Protector" and "Meadowlark," aren't that meaningful lyrically—they're not trying to make any broader point. The words are just loosely arranged imagery there to support the music. When writing the lyrics for the album *Helplessness Blues*, I'd often think back on the failings of these two songs specifically. I didn't want to just throw words together anymore, I wanted to say something.

# BLUE RIDGE MOUNTAINS
FLEET FOXES / 04:25

# BLUE RIDGE MOUNTAINS[1]

Lie down[2] with me my dear, lie down
Under stormy night, tell nobody

My brother, where do you intend to go tonight?
I heard that you missed your connecting flight[3]
To the Blue Ridge Mountains, over near Tennessee[4]

You're ever welcome with me anytime you like
Let's drive to the countryside, leave behind some green-eyed look-alikes[5]
So no one gets worried, no
So no one gets worried, no

---

*Can we save the best part of the song for the second half? How can we arrive there?*

1. People from this region still bring this song up to me as being formative for them and important to them, and I always feel weird about it, because I had never really been to the Blue Ridge Mountains at this point in my life. I have since then, but at the time they were just a symbol for something far-off and unknown, like Mykonos.

2. Why is this guy always lying down? Sounds lazy.

3. This is pretty much the only lyrical moment on the album that references the post-industrial era.

4. Tennessee #2.

5. I'm incredibly close with my brother. He's the best.

But Sean, don't get careless
I'm sure it'll be fine
I love you, I love you
O brother of mine

In the quivering forest
Where the shivering dog rests
Our good grandfather
Built a wooden nest[6]
And the river got frozen
And the home got snowed in
And a yellow moon glowed bright
Till the morning light

Terrible am I, child
Even if you don't mind

---

6. This is true—in the seventies, my mom's dad built a small log cabin on a river in eastern Washington. It was a nexus for the whole family for decades of gatherings and events and remains so, long after his passing. My nine-year-old cousin once removed recently told me this was her favorite song because "It's about the cabin."

In the quivering forest
Where the shivering dog rests
Our good grandfather
Built a wooden nest
And the river got frozen
And the home got snowed in
And a yellow moon glowed bright
Till the morning light

Terrible am I, child
Even if you don't mind

# OLIVER JAMES
FLEET FOXES / 03:23

# OLIVER JAMES[1]

On the way to your brother's house in the valley deep
By the river bridge a cradle, floating beside me
In the whitest water on the bank against the stone
You will lift his body from the shore and bring him home

Oliver James, washed in the rain no longer
Oliver James, washed in the rain no longer

On the kitchen table that your grandfather did make
You in your delicate way will slowly clean his face
And you will remember when you rehearsed the actions of
An innocent and anxious mother full of anxious love

Oliver James, washed in the rain no longer
Oliver James, washed in the rain no longer

---

*Can I write a song that will be mostly one voice a cappella live and pull it off?*

1. Like "White Winter Hymnal," which some people think to be about decapitation, I've been asked if this song is about abortion or stillbirth. To me, it's pretty obviously just a version of the finding of Moses in the ark of bulrushes.

Walk with me down Ruby Beach[2] and through the valley floor
Love for the one you know more
Love for the one you know more

Back we go to your brother's house, emptier my dear
The sound of ancient voices ringing soft upon your ear

Oliver James,[3] washed in the rain no longer
Oliver James, washed in the rain no longer

---

2. Except Moses here is on the Olympic Peninsula in Washington State.

3. And he is named Oliver James.

# UNRELEASED
## MARCH 2011

· I'M LOSING MYSELF ·
· DERWENTWATER STONES ·

# I'M LOSING MYSELF

UNRELEASED / 03:26

# I'M LOSING MYSELF[1]

I'm a fast breather
I'm a hairless dog
And alone at the end of the day, I am just like the gathering fog[2]
I'm a slow mover
I'm the best-laid plans
And alone at the end of the day, I just sit with my head in my hands
But we speak easy
And we seldom fight
And I chew on the bones of the day
While you sleep soft and warm in the night
And I can't see you with anyone else
Even if that means holding me down, even if that means losing myself

---

*When will this damn album be done?*

1. This song is a duet with Ed Droste of the amazing band Grizzly Bear, a group of musicians I've admired and looked up to since their very first releases. We were deep in the weeds of making *Helplessness Blues* at the time, attempting to follow up the unexpected success of the first album, and I was feeling very in-over-my-head.

2. I remember sitting in the live room at Sear Sound in Hell's Kitchen, New York City, despondent, writing this song as Phil Ek tried to mix the abandoned early version of *Helplessness Blues*. We went to mix the album too soon, long before it was actually finished.

He's a smooth talker
And he shaves his face
And I wonder if you look at me and instead see him taking my place
But I do need you, and no one else
And I hope you're around and forgiving
When you see me losing myself

# DERWENTWATER STONES

UNRELEASED / 03:23

# DERWENTWATER STONES[1]

Midnight in the swaying leaves
Midnight in the field
And the moon is like a sheet
Covering the shield

And you told me come along
Carrying no weight
To the Derwentwater stones
And I know the place

All the faces in the moss
Look like those I've known
Or like bruises on the rocks
On the broken stone

---

*Can I make a song that Bert Jansch could have covered?*

1. On the hiking trip in the English Lake District I mentioned earlier, my brother and I chanced upon a standing stone circle, like a miniature Stonehenge, in a pasture near to Derwentwater, a principal lake of the region. This song is just an evocation of that memory.

And the voices speak to me
And the faces change
And the rhododendron seeds
Bloom and stain the range

And you tell me to be good
Now I'm on my own
Through the red and auburn wood
To the broken stone

Midnight in the swaying leaves
Midnight in the field
And the moon is like a sheet
Covering the shield

# HELPLESSNESS BLUES
## MAY 3, 2011

· MONTEZUMA · BEDOUIN DRESS · SIM SALA BIM ·
· BATTERY KINZIE · THE PLAINS / BITTER DANCER ·
· HELPLESSNESS BLUES · LORELAI · SOMEONE YOU'D ADMIRE ·
· THE SHRINE / AN ARGUMENT · BLUE SPOTTED TAIL ·
· GROWN OCEAN ·

# MONTEZUMA
HELPLESSNESS BLUES / 03:36

# MONTEZUMA

So now I am older
Than my mother and father
When they had their daughter
Now what does that say about me?[1]

O how could I dream of
Such a selfless and true love
Could I wash my hands of
Just looking out for me

O man, what I used to be[2]
O man o my o me
O man, what I used to be
O man o my o me

---

*Can I confront what scares me?*

1. This verse sets up the existential questions of the whole album: the anxieties of the onset of adulthood, the paradox of measuring oneself against parents who came of age in a completely different social and political era.

2. Some context for this line: I look exactly like my dad. The line still makes sense otherwise, but that's the intended subtext.

In dearth or in excess
Both the slave and the empress
Will return to the dirt, I guess
Naked as when they came

I wonder if I'll see
Any faces above me
Or just cracks in the ceiling
Nobody else to blame

Gold teeth and gold jewelry
Every piece of your dowry
Throw them into the tomb with me
Bury them with my name
Unless I have somebody
Ran my wandering mind away

O man, what I used to be
Montezuma to Tripoli[3]
O man, O my, O me

---

3. Reference to "The Marines' Hymn" of the United States Marine Corps. My father
served in the Coast Guard in his twenties; I never served my country.

# BEDOUIN DRESS
## HELPLESSNESS BLUES / 04:30

# BEDOUIN DRESS

If to borrow is to take and not return
I have borrowed all my lonesome life[1]
And I can't, no I can't get through
The borrower's debt is the only regret of my youth

And believe me, it's not easy when I look back
Everything I took I'd soon return
Just to be at Innisfree again
All of the sirens are driving me over the stern
Just to be at Innisfree again
All of the sirens are driving me over the stern

One day at Innisfree[2]
One day that's mine there

---

*Can we build a song around a circular riff and a wordless chorus?*

1. Following the success of the first Fleet Foxes album, one of the things I found myself preoccupied with was artistic influence and indebtedness. Some people were reducing the music to "x old artist meets y old artist," and I became confused about the creative process, feeling almost a guilt around borrowing from musicians I loved.

2. On a wall at the cabin my grandfather built, my grandmother had framed the text of the poem "The Lake Isle of Innisfree," by W. B. Yeats.

In the street one day I saw you among the crowd
In a geometric patterned dress
Gleaming white just as I recalled
Old as I get I would never forget it at all
Gleaming white just as I recalled
Old as I get I could never forget it at all

One day at Innisfree
One day that's mine there

# SIM SALA BIM

HELPLESSNESS BLUES / 03:14

# SIM SALA BIM

He was so kind, such a gentleman tied to the oceanside[1]
Lighting a match on the suitcase's latch in the fading of night
Ruffled the fur of the collie 'neath the table[2]
Ran out the door through the dark
Carved out his initials in the bark

Then the Earth shook, that was all that it took for the dream to break
All the loose ends would surround me again in the shape of your face
What makes me love you despite the reservations
What do I see in your eyes
Besides my reflection hanging high?

Are you off somewhere reciting incantations,
"Sim sala bim" on your tongue,
Carving off the hair of someone's young?

---

*What is a guitar solo in folk music?*

1. In some ways, this song is an appreciative ode to Magnus Toren, the proprietor of the Henry Miller Memorial Library in Big Sur, California, a place we've been lucky to play and visit and break bread at many times over the years.

2. First and only appearance of a dog in the catalog. This moment was singled out by *NME* as especially twee in a lukewarm review of this album.

Remember when you had me cut your hair?
Call me Delilah then
I wouldn't care

# BATTERY KINZIE
## HELPLESSNESS BLUES / 02:50

# BATTERY KINZIE[1]

I woke up one morning
All my fingers rotting
I woke up a dying man without a chance

I came to your window
Threw a stone and waited
At the door a stranger stood
The stranger's voice said nothing good
I turned to walk the frozen ground alone
All the way home

---

*Can there be at least \*one\* upbeat song on this album?*

1. Battery Kinzie is the name of a structure at Fort Worden, an old military installation in Port Townsend, Washington, constructed at the beginning of the twentieth century to protect the Puget Sound from possible Pacific or Canadian invasion. That invasion never came, and the base has been repurposed in various ways over the years. My parents ran a small film festival at the old theater there in the seventies, and it has been a home to artists, craftspeople, and creatives ever since. Some of the most cavernous reverb on *Helplessness Blues* was recorded underneath Fort Worden, in a drained water cistern.

Wide-eyed walker
Do not wander
Do not wander
Through the dawn

Both my eyes are fading
No light in the evening
Planted like a seed in sand
And drowned in rain
Watch you for an hour
He kept you beneath him
He kept you on lock and key
He paid the wage you sent to me
And wastes the day so idly alone
All the way home

Wide-eyed walker
Do not wander
Do not wander
Through the dawn

Wide-eyed walker
Do not wander
Do not wander
Through the dawn

# THE PLAINS /
# BITTER DANCER
HELPLESSNESS BLUES / 05:54

# THE PLAINS /
# BITTER DANCER[1]

Just as the sand made everything round
Just as the tar seeps up from the ground
Bitter dancer, ever turning
So was the day that you came to town

You took a room and you settled in
Washed off the chalk from your weathered skin
Daylight sleeper, bloody reaper
You took a room and you settled in

I should have known one day you would come
All of us walk so blind in the sun
Midnight feeder, beggar pleader
I should have known one day you would come

---

*How many voices and individual vocal lines can we layer in this intro?*

1. There was a period following the success of the first album when I didn't really know who I could trust. I got burned a couple of times mistaking opportunism as kindness and kind of shrank away from people for a time.

Tell me again my only son
Tell me again, what have you done?

At arm's length
I will hold you there

At arm's length
I will hold you there

# HELPLESSNESS BLUES

HELPLESSNESS BLUES / 05:02

# HELPLESSNESS BLUES[1]

I was raised up believing I was somehow unique
Like a snowflake distinct among snowflakes
Unique in each way you'd conceive
And now after some thinking, I'd say I'd rather be
A functioning cog in some great machinery
Serving something beyond me
But I don't, I don't know what that will be
I'll get back to you someday soon, you will see

What's my name? What's my station?

---

*Can I be so emotionally direct that it's actually uncomfortable? Can a song be half rousing and half dreamlike?*

1. This is the song that the band is probably best known for at this point. It's clearly written from the perspective of a confused kid, full of energy and passion but unsure of their place in the world, unsure where they belong. It predates the use of "snowflake" as an epithet against liberals, itself a trend hopefully left behind in the Trump years. I meant every word of this song, and still struggle with the same feelings, so I understand why it connected with listeners, but it leaves me in a vulnerable position of feeling too seen and having been too emotionally revealing.

O just tell me what I should do
I don't need to be kind to the armies of night
That would do such injustice to you
Or bow down and be grateful and say
"Sure, take all that you see"
To the men who move only in dimly lit halls
And determine my future for me
And I don't, I don't know who to believe
I'll get back to you someday soon, you will see

If I know only one thing, it's that everything that I see
Of the world outside is so inconceivable
Often I barely can speak
Yeah I'm tongue-tied and dizzy
And I can't keep it to myself
What good is it to sing helplessness blues?
Why should I wait for anyone else?
And I know, I know you will keep me on the shelf
I'll come back to you someday soon, myself

If I had an orchard, I'd work till I'm raw
If I had an orchard, I'd work till I'm sore[2]
And you would wait tables and soon run the store
Gold hair in the sunlight, my light in the dawn
If I had an orchard, I'd work till I'm sore
If I had an orchard, I'd work till I'm sore
Someday I'll be like the man on the screen[3]

---

2. "If I had an orchard"—still sung to me from people passing by in cars—was intended to be an update on "If I had a hammer." I felt more like cultivating than smashing.

3. One reason this song makes me feel dumb is that every problem this lyric proposes is quite easily solved by this incredibly beautiful thing I am so lucky and grateful to still get to do: make music, perform music, support other musicians, commune with other music fans and supporters. It's like writing "I'm lost" over and over again on a map of the way out, to the point that you can't see the route anymore. D'oh.

# LORELAI

HELPLESSNESS BLUES / 04:25

# LORELAI

So, guess I got old
I was like trash on the sidewalk[1]
I guess I knew why
Often it's hard to just sweet talk

I was old news to you then
Old news, old news to you then

You, you were like glue
Holding each of us together
I slept through July
While you made lines in the heather

I was old news to you then
Old news, old news to you then
Fell for the ruse with you then
Old news, old news to you then

---

*Was Dylan's "Fourth Time Around" good enough the first time, really?*

1. Like the "connecting flight" in "Blue Ridge Mountains," here's another tenuous connection to lived reality.

And I still see you when I try to sleep
I see the garden, the tower, the street
Call out to nobody, call out to me
Chip on the shoulder, the diamond, the teeth

Now I can see how
We were like dust on the window
Not much, not a lot
Everything stolen or borrowed[2]

I was old news to you then
Old news, old news to you then

---

2. The borrowing fixation from "Bedouin Dress" appears again.

# SOMEONE
# YOU'D ADMIRE
HELPLESSNESS BLUES / 02:30

# SOMEONE YOU'D ADMIRE[1]

After all is said and done I feel the same
All that I hoped would change within me stayed
Like a huddled moonlit exile on the shore
Warming his hands a thousand years ago

I walk with others in me yearning to get out
Claw at my skin and gnash their teeth and shout
One of them wants only to be someone you'd admire
One would as soon just throw you on the fire

After all is said and after all is done
God only knows which of them I'll become

---

*What song can I find in the tuning CGCGCC?*

1. This song was deeply inspired by the great English folk singer Nic Jones, a masterful
interpreter of standards and a fantastic guitar player.

# THE SHRINE /
# AN ARGUMENT
## HELPLESSNESS BLUES / 08:06

# THE SHRINE /
# AN ARGUMENT[1]

I went down among the dust and pollen
To the old stone fountain in the morning after dawn
Underneath were all these pennies fallen
From the hands of children
They were there and then were gone

And I wonder what became of them
What became of them
Sunlight over me, no matter what I do

Apples in the summer, all cold and sweet
Every day a'passing complete

---

*How many songs can I fit in one song?*

1. My attempt at writing a very long, epic song, inspired by Joanna Newsom's incredible run of albums. I remember getting this song together to debut while opening for her on tour in 2010. After the first show she said, "How old are you!?" and when I said, "Twenty-four," she, in the most loving and hilarious way, scoffed! Still the best thing that's ever happened to me.

I'm not one to ever pray for mercy
Or to wish on pennies in the fountain or the shrine
But that day you know I left my money
And I thought of you only
All that copper glowing fine

And I wonder what became of you
What became of you
Sunlight over me no matter what I do

Apples in the summer, all cold and sweet
Every day a' passing complete
Apples in the summer, all cold and sweet
Every day a' passing complete

In the morning, waking up to terrible sunlight
All diffuse like skin abused the sun is half its size
When you talk you hardly even look in my eyes
In the morning, in the morning

In the doorway holding every letter that I wrote
In the driveway pulling away, putting on your coat
In the ocean washing off my name from your throat
In the morning, in the morning
In the ocean washing off my name from your throat
In the morning, in the morning

Green apples hang from my tree
They belong only to me

Green apples hang from my green apple tree
They belong only to, only to me
And if I just stay awhile here staring at the sea
And the waves break ever closer, ever near to me
I will lay down in the sand and let the ocean lead
Carry me to Innisfree like pollen on the breeze

# BLUE SPOTTED TAIL

HELPLESSNESS BLUES / 03:05

# BLUE SPOTTED TAIL<sup>1</sup>

Why in the night sky are the lights hung?
Why is the Earth moving round the sun?
Floating in the vacuum with no purpose, not a one
Why in the night sky are the lights hung?

Why is life made only for to end?
Why do I do all this waiting then?
Why this frightened part of me that's fated to pretend?
Why is life made only for to end?

In the city only for a while
Here to face the fortune and the bile
I heard you on the radio, I couldn't help but smile
In the city only for a while

---

*What if Kierkegaard wrote a nursery rhyme?*

1. Sometimes people tell me they sing this song to their children at bedtime, and it's such a beautiful image, but there's a pessimism to the lyrics that makes it hard for me to imagine singing it to a kid of my own. Maybe someday.

Why in the night sky are the lights hung?
Why is the Earth moving round the sun?
Floating in the vacuum with no purpose, not a one
Why in the night sky are the lights hung?

# GROWN OCEAN
## HELPLESSNESS BLUES / 04:36

# GROWN OCEAN[1]

In that dream, I'm as old as the mountains
Still as starlight reflected in fountains, then
Children grown on the edge of the ocean
Kept like jewelry, kept with devotion
In that dream, moving slow through the morning time

You would come to me then, without answers
Lick my wounds and remove my demands for now
Eucalyptus and orange trees are blooming
In that dream, there's no darkness a'looming
In that dream, moving slow through the morning time

In that dream I could hardly contain it
All my life I will wait to attain it, then

---

*Is there hope, after all?*

1. After all of the existential questioning on this album, it ends with an idealized dream of the future: living happily, raising children, questions answered. As in the song "Helplessness Blues," I wanted to inflect some of the idealism with flashes of realism, questions about whether this idealized dream were possible.

I know someday the smoke will all burn off
All these voices I'll someday have turned off, then
I will see you someday when I've woken
I'll be so happy just to have spoken
I'll have so much to tell you about it then

In that dream I could hardly contain it
All my life I will wait to attain it, then

Wide-eyed walker, don't betray me
I will wake one day, don't delay me
Wide-eyed leaver, always going

# CRACK-UP
## JUNE 16, 2017

· I AM ALL THAT I NEED / ARROYO SECO / THUMBPRINT SCAR ·
· CASSIUS, – · – NAIADS, CASSADIES ·
· KEPT WOMAN · THIRD OF MAY / ŌDAIGAHARA ·
· IF YOU NEED TO, KEEP TIME ON ME · MEARCSTAPA ·
· ON ANOTHER OCEAN (JANUARY / JUNE) · FOOL'S ERRAND ·
· I SHOULD SEE MEMPHIS · CRACK-UP ·

# I AM ALL THAT I NEED / ARROYO SECO / THUMBPRINT SCAR

CRACK-UP / 06:25

# I AM ALL THAT I NEED /
# ARROYO SECO /
# THUMBPRINT SCAR

[I am all that I need
And I'll be till I'm through
And I'm light on my feet
Good to be without you
Distant light, distant dancer
Mute at midnight, she might look like the answer
But I'm all that I need][1]

So it's true I've gone too far to find you
And the thumbprint scar I let define you
Was a myth I made you measure up to
It was all just water, winding by you[2]

---

*What would it sound like if a song frequently transitioned between micro and macro scales, in terms of production and delivery?*

1. On this song and album I began playing with my vocal register, singing as low and quiet as my voice would allow for some sections and as high and impassioned as it would allow for others. I thought of a register shift as a scene change in a movie, a depiction of a different place, and built songs that juxtaposed those interiors and exteriors.

2. After the bald, questioning introspection of *Helplessness Blues*, I retreated somewhat into coded language. I wanted to make music but I didn't want to feel seen.

And the basking, gnashing, foaling, feeding
And the rising, falling, melting, freezing
And the raising for destroying feeling
[All we do, this repeats!][3]
You've got all you need on me!

And now I see that it's all corroding
Soonest seething, soonest folding
But the night won't last if you just hold fast, so calm down

[I am hardly made of steel]
Tell me are you so concealed?
[Can't I just go to sleep?]
You're no more so blind to me[4]

Are you alone?
I don't believe you
Are you at home? I'll come right now
I need to see you
Thin as a shim and Scottish pale
Bright white light like a bridal veil
"I don't need you" cut to chewn-through fingernails

---

3. Subconscious, inner-monologue interjection, sung in an inverse vocal register.

4. Sonically and lyrically, this is a conversation between two halves of a divided self.

I was a child in the ivy then
I never knew you, you knew me
Not like you knew me
Off on the other ocean, now
All is behind you, all is sea

# CASSIUS, –
CRACK-UP / 04:50

# CASSIUS, –[1]

Past my window, out in the street
Life makes short work of all I see
Men take the change from beggars[2]
Tight bound in sheets
Red and blue, the useless sirens scream[3]

Song of masses, passing outside
All inciting the fifth of July
When guns for hire opened fire[4]
Blind against the dawn
When the knights in iron took the pawn
You and I, out into the night
Held within the line that they have drawn

---

*Can I build a musical instrument out of samples of my own voice, and build a song around it?*

1. Cassius the conspirator, the protestor, and a slight nod to the birth name of Muhammad Ali.

2. Change being coins, or change being Change.

3. Sirens scream as in the *Odyssey*, or sirens scream as in enhanced police presence.

4. A reference to protests following the shooting of Alton Sterling by police in Baton Rouge, July 5, 2016.

As I went they're all beside us in silence[5]
As if unaffected amid the violence
O, are we all so tamed?
I was in a river as if in water
Wife, a son, a son, a son and a daughter[6]
O, are we all so tamed?

I walked home, no words to say
Cassius one month gone on his way
And who will lead us, and who remains to die?[7]
By a thread, drop my head to cry

As I went they're all beside us in silence
As if unaffected amid the violence
O, are we all so tamed?
I was in a river as if in water
Wife, a son, a son, a son and a daughter
O, are we all so tamed?

---

5. Reference to the phenomenon of protest marches being escorted by police: the mute presence of the very system that is being protested, the futility this phenomenon suggests.

6. The metaphorical left-behind, families ruined following rupture.

7. I wrote this in 2016—if we only knew.

# – NAIADS, CASSADIES

CRACK-UP / 03:10

# – NAIADS, CASSADIES[1]

Who stole the life from you?
Who turned you so against you?
Who was the thief, who shaved your teeth
Accepting just virtue?

And did he act alone?
Were any more complicit?
When he would sing, and offer the ring
What older voice said, "Kiss it"?

Who?

---

*Can we chill out for a second?*

1. This song was about the way we can give so much of our power away to others, and hold their opinions above our own, and how our perceptions of our potential can really cloud us and define our lives. We need some degree of self-definition, but we can also end up deeply out of touch with what we naturally are, in favor of trying to attain some externally derived ideal.

Fire can't doubt its heat
Water can't doubt its power
You're not adrift
You're not a gift
You know you're not a flower

# KEPT WOMAN

CRACK-UP / 03:55

# KEPT WOMAN[1]

Anna you're lost in a shadow there
Cinder and smoke hanging in the air
O and I know you'll be
Bolder than me
I was high, I was unaware

God above saw, ever in the mind
Blue and white irises in a line
Under your nameless shame
I left you in frame, and you rose to be ossified
As a rose of the oceanside

---

*What would a bad trip sound like?*

1. An example of a song that means a lot to me, but whose meaning would be totally unclear to anyone else. This song is about the first and only time I have done psychedelic mushrooms. I was alone in my backyard in Portland, Oregon, and someone had left a small bag of mushrooms at my house. I was about to move across the country to go back to school, so with little to lose, I decided to eat the mushrooms. Bad idea! I ended up tearing out all of the vegetables from my garden, strewing them across the yard, professing my love to my neighbor across the fence, and falling asleep in the grass after a couple hours of laughing uncontrollably. Never again!

Too long till the light of the morning
So unseen, as light in a dream
Too long now to the rising
Too long now to the rising

Can you be slow for a little while?
Widow your soul for another mile?
I'm just the same as when
You saw me back then
And we're bound to be reconciled
We're bound to be reconciled

Too long swinging the knife
All will wash over you, in a night so unending
Not long now to the rising
Not long now to the rising

Anna you're lost in a shadow there
Cinder and smoke hanging in the air
Oh and I know you'll be
Bolder than me
I was high, I was unaware

# THIRD OF MAY /
# ŌDAIGAHARA
CRACK-UP / 08:49

# THIRD OF MAY / ŌDAIGAHARA

Light ended the night, but the song remained
And I was hiding by the stair, half here, half there
Past the lashing rain
And as the sky would petal white, old innocent lies came to mind
As we stood, congregated, at the firing line[1]

Night ended the fight, but the song remained
And so I headed to the wall
Turned tail to call to the new domain
As if in the sight of sea, you're suddenly free
But it's all the same
Oh, but I can hear you, loud in the center
Aren't we made to be crowded together, like leaves?[2]

---

*What would a travelogue of the last ten years of our lives sound like?*

1. Ekphrastic allusion to Francisco Goya's painting *The Third of May 1808.*

2. The year 2020 answered "no."

151

[Was I too slow?
Did you change overnight?
Second son, on the other line][3]

Now, back in our town as a castaway
I'm reminded of the time it all fell in line
On the third of May
As if it were designed
Painted in sand to be washed away
Oh but I can hear you, loud in the center
Aren't we made to be crowded together, like leaves?

[Was I too slow?
Did I change overnight?
Second son, for the second time]

Can I be light and free?
If I lead you through the fury, will you call to me?
And is all that I might owe you carved on ivory?

But all will fade, all I say, all I needed
As a flash in the eye, I wouldn't deny, all receded

---

3. Another tangential aside presented in an inverse vocal register.

Life unfolds in pools of gold
I am only owed this shape if I make a line to hold
To be held within one's self is deathlike, oh I know

But all will be, for mine and me, as we make it
And the size of the fray can't take it away, they won't make it

[I was a fool
Crime after crime to confess to
But I hold the fleet angel, she'll bless you
Hold fast to the wing
Hold fast to the wing][4]

---

4. The third of May means a few things in Fleet Foxes world—it's the birthday of both Skyler Skjelset and Josh Tillman, and it's the day that the album *Helplessness Blues* was released. When I first saw Goya's Third of May, which depicts a line of rebels facing a firing squad, it also looked to me like a band standing before an audience, and the song came to be a bit of a "story-so-far" of our experience making music in the world together. It begins as a great adventure, dovetails into periods of strife and peace, and ends in a cloud of warm ambiguity.

# IF YOU NEED TO, KEEP TIME ON ME

CRACK-UP / 03:30

# IF YOU NEED TO, KEEP TIME ON ME[1]

How could it all fall in one day?
Were we too sure of the sun?

If you need to, keep time on me
If you need to, keep time on me

Who knows what state is in store?
If they all turn, will you run?

If you need to, keep time on me
If you need to, keep time on me

When I need to, I'll keep time on you

---

*Can we make a good counterbalance to the most intense song on the album, so the track list flows well?*

1. This was recorded the day after Trump was elected. I'd already written some of the lyrics, but they took on new meaning in the context of an uncertain political future that seemed quite bleak. There was a sense that we would need to stick together and rely on community to get through the Trump years, and there was no foreknowledge of how impossible that would become in year four.

White oceans roar
A frightened fool stokes heedless fire[2]

But if you need to, keep time on me
If you need to, keep time on me

How could it all fall in one day?
Were we too sure of the sun?

If you need to, keep time on me
If you need to, keep time on me[3]

---

2. "White" and "heedless" are homophonic with "wide" and "heatless."

3. The soothing, balmy repetitions of the refrain are meant to evoke the promise of reliability in the words.

# MEARCSTAPA
CRACK-UP / 04:10

# MEARCSTAPA[1]

Two lines in the air
Two eyes on the pair[2]
Mearcstapa, on an open sea
But you turn away
No falling today
No wind in the night
You're putting slack in the lines

The eyes of the sea
So easy to meet
Mearcstapa, deaf and blind like me
But the foam doesn't sing
The phone doesn't ring
So what will you find
Mearcstapa of mine?

---

*What song can I find in the tuning GADFAC? Can I make a vocal melody that accommodates strange chordal modulations?*

1. An Old English compound word meaning roughly "border-walker" that's found only in *Beowulf.*

2. These lines are describing the music itself.

161

# ON ANOTHER OCEAN
# (JANUARY / JUNE)
## CRACK-UP / 04:24

# ON ANOTHER OCEAN
# (JANUARY / JUNE)[1]

Biding your time on the other ocean
Falling into line in the cold and dim
Wherever you run, you see all you leave behind you
Lies inside anyone you open
On the other ocean
On the other ocean
On the other ocean

Was he not quite as you had conceived him?
Did the color of the light hide the fight in the eyes?
Wherever you run, you see only eyes behind you
Lies inside anyone you open
On the other ocean
On the other ocean
On the other ocean
On the other ocean

---

*How can we use anticipation and transition to maximize a song's frissonic effect?*

1. During this period of my life I had kind of fled to New York City and tried to live a very different life, recovering from some stressors in early adulthood and unsure of what to do next. I lived through some particularly brutal winters contrasted with some particularly beautiful springs, and this song was an attempt to depict that almost bipolar dichotomy.

So do you think the smoke it won't enfold you?
Or there'll be someone waiting for you
Off in the distance, then?

If only anything could change you
If only you knew what you claim to
If only every sign you cling to
If only they were so

Turn any eye into the ivy
And I won't bleed out if I know me
All I need, oh don't deny me
You ended up too strained
Oh I would lead it in the morning
Oh I won't even if I know it
All I need, oh don't deny me
We're in the eye sometimes

Too young
Too young

# FOOL'S ERRAND

CRACK-UP / 04:48

# FOOL'S ERRAND[1]

I knew you fine
Sight dream of mine
But I know my eyes, they've often lied
And I move like blood, like fire and flood
Despite you

Blind love couldn't win
As the facts all came in
And I know I'll again chase after wind
What have I got if not a thought?

I knew, oh I knew
I knew

---

*What would a George Jones song covered by the Electric Prunes sound like?*

1. Another song concerned with the difference between perception and reality. For myself and many musicians I know, choosing this life was about embracing an idealistic, romanticized notion of how life can be—the adventure of traveling, performing, creating, connecting, living without a safety net, fully invested, fully committed. At times the life of a musician feels that way, but it also involves as much drudgery and strife as many other life paths. It ends up being about balancing the idealism and zest that seem necessary for making good music with the realism required to be a functioning person in society.

It was a fool's errand
Waiting for a sign
But I can't leave until the sight comes to mind
A fool's errand

Life will repeat, vision I see
The mouth and the teeth
And that's fine with me
What have I got if not a thought?

I knew, oh I knew
I knew

It was a fool's errand
Waiting for a sign
But I can't leave until the sight comes to mind
A fool's errand

But I can make it through
I was thin and I saw all life in you
Fool's errand

# I SHOULD
# SEE MEMPHIS
CRACK-UP / 04:44

# I SHOULD SEE MEMPHIS[1]

Endless vacation felt like perdition
Sybarite woman stood at attention[2]
Pacing the basement like Cassius in Rome
Or in Kinshasa, just let me at him
Like First Manassas, like Appomattox[3]
I've got my teeth in it, I won't let go

[But I gave you no option
Illusion of choosing
And if you wouldn't stop them,
Then you just hate losing]

---

*How low can I sing?*

1. I wanted every line of this song to refute the line before it in some way. Memphis meaning the city in Tennessee, but also the Naiad nymph Memphis of Greek myth, wife of Epaphus and co-founder of Memphis, Egypt.

2. A lackadaisical, slothful first line, a militaristic and active second.

3. Among the first and last battles of the American Civil War.

I miss the highway
I should see Memphis
She sees it my way
Her and Osiris[4]

4. I remember being—shocker—incredibly confused while making this album, and deciding at some point that instead of treating that confusion as a bug, I'd try and make it a feature. Whereas *Helplessness Blues* told about it, *Crack-Up* showed it.

# CRACK-UP

CRACK-UP / 06:24

# CRACK-UP[1]

So the mind won't lie
And the arm won't set
And the bright red eye
Isn't off you yet

So the words won't come
And the hand won't touch
And a midnight sun
Doesn't look like much

As an iris contracts,
Facing the day

---

*Can a song feel like being on a ship getting torn apart by an iceberg?*

1. The title of this album came from F. Scott Fitzgerald's seminal essay "The Crack-Up," where he describes feeling cracked in a way that wasn't possible to recover from. I identified with this at the time. I'd convinced myself that musical success had come too easily, so I found as many ways to make my life difficult as I could—retreat into isolation, live on the top floor of seven-story walk-up with few possessions, read *Ulysses*, spend most of my time alone, run five to ten miles a day, build inscrutable sonic worlds founded on arcane presuppositions . . . happy to be on the other side of that now, but I also think *Crack-Up* is my favorite Fleet Foxes album. I'll leave the begged question of whether one has to suffer for their art for a later book.

I can tell you've cracked
Like a china plate

When the world insists
That the false is so
With a philippic, as Cicero
The tighter the fist,
The looser the sand

If I don't resist,
Will I understand?

All things change, dividing tides
Far as I can see
All fades through
But a light of you
As Ylajali

All I see
Dividing tides
Rising over me

# SHORE
## SEPTEMBER 22, 2020

# WADING IN
# WAIST-HIGH WATER
SHORE / 02:15

# WADING IN WAIST-HIGH WATER[1]

Summer all over
Blame it on timing
Weakening August water
Loose-eyed in morning
Sunlight covered over
Wading in sight of fire

And we're finally aligning
More than maybe I can choose

Soon as I knew you
All so wide open
Wading inside of fire
As if I just saw you
Cross Second Avenue
Wading in waist-high water

---

*Can a song feel like a prelude, a warm summer day, and a fever dream all at once?*

1. This song is sung by the immensely talented Uwade Akhere, the first time another vocalist has sung lead on a Fleet Foxes song. I thought it worked as a surreal, dreamlike prelude to the album itself. Thank you, Uwade!

And I love you so violent
More than maybe I can do

Now we're finally aligning
More than maybe I can choose

# SUNBLIND
SHORE / 04:13

# SUNBLIND[1]

For[2] Richard Swift
For John and Bill
For every gift lifted far before its will[3]
Judee and Smith
For Berman too[4]
I've met the myth[5] hanging heavy over you
I loved you long
You rose to go
Beneath you, songs, perfect angels in the snow[6]

---

*What if I could write only one more song?*

1. That dazed feeling one gets from staring too long at something too bright, which is how I usually feel after listening to too much good music.

2. I wanted the first word I sang on "album four" to be "for."

3. These artists were gifts and remain gifts!

4. Richard Swift, John Prine, Bill Withers, Judee Sill, Elliott Smith, David Berman—dear departed heroes.

5. The myth here would be the mythology surrounding lost musicians, the veneration of their absence, which I've met sideways at times in this life in music.

6. An allusion to both David Berman's poem "Snow" and Elliott Smith's song "Angels in the Snow."

So time to stage[7]
Forget reserve
The type of great coronation you deserve

I'm going out for a weekend
I'm gonna borrow a Martin or Gibson
With *Either/Or* and *The Hex* for my *Bookends*
Carrying every text that you've given[8]

I'm gonna swim for a week in
Warm *American Water*[9] with dear friends
Swimming high on a lea in an Eden[10]
Running all of the leads you've been leaving

---

7. "Time to stage" being a bit of concert lingo that these artists would have been familiar with.

8. I used to try to hide my influences, or was ashamed of them, which was some combination of impostor syndrome and pride. In thinking about this song as the musical equivalent of the phone call to a loved one you might make from a crashing plane, there was only really room for honoring influences and saying thank you, admitting and embracing how influence-ridden we are, can be, and really should be.

9. *American Water* being an album by Silver Jews, David Berman's band.

10. For the chorus, the language shifts to the natural—we've driven past the graveyard and arrived at the swimming hole.

I'm overmatched (for Arthur Russell)[11]
I'm half as wise (Duncan and Curtis)
If this is flat, brother, I apologize (Jimi and David, for Nick and Otis)
No one alone (for Bell and Buckley)
Can leave the cave (Marvin and Adam)
And all you've loaned won't be kept inside a grave[12] (for Arthur Russell,
for Arthur Russell)

I'm gonna swim for a week in
Warm *American Water* with dear friends
Just intending that I would delight them[13]
Swimming high on a lea in an Eden

So I dream, dream
So I dream, dream

---

11. Protestration, lest one assume the drawing of false equivalency.

12. The immortality they've achieved in their art.

13. I used to think about music-making solely as personal expression or a chasing of curiosity, but now the most generative aspect of it to me is the chance to make something that might make someone else's day, the same way these artists have carried me through so much over the years.

I'm gonna swim for a week in
Warm *American Water* with dear friends
Swimming high on a lea in an Eden
Running all of the leads you've been leaving[14]
And in your rarified air I feel sunblind
I'm looking up at you there high in my mind
Only way that I made it for a long time
But I'm loud and alive, singing you all night, night

Warm *American Water*

---

14. Leaving / leaving behind.

# CAN I BELIEVE YOU

SHORE / 04:04

# CAN I BELIEVE YOU[1]

Can I believe you?
Can I believe you?
Can I ever know your mind?
Am I handing you mine?
Do we both confide?

I see it, eat through every word I sow
See what you need to, do you doubt it's yours?
Now I'm learning the ropes
Never get this close
I've been wounded before
Hasn't let me go

It never got less strange, showing anyone just a bare face[2]
If I don't, well, nothing will change
Staying under my weather all day

---

*Can I smuggle an odd time signature into a pop song and have it feel natural?*

1. This is yet another song where the lyric bloomed from vocalese gibberish, and I had to take what was given and figure it out from there. The register this song is sung in has certain emotional and phonemic strictures and it was a struggle to put together.

2. People think of Fleet Foxes as a quintessential "beard band." I just hate how I look without one.

Can I believe you when you say I'm good
I didn't need to when I wished you would
No it isn't enough
Never held that much
Now another way up
Been a row too rough

It never got less strange, showing anyone just a bare face
If I don't, well, nothing will change
Staying under my weather all day

Lately, I'm wondering too
What type of desire I can break
When I'm one way with them, one with you
What half is it of me rearranged?

Can I believe you?
Can I believe you?
I want to need you
I want to need you
Can I believe you?
Can I believe you?

# JARA
SHORE / 04:09

# JARA[1]

First sight of the first good morning since you've been out of town
First time any violet omens don't shadow me around
So you want part of the great white tyrant, of ghost after ghost?
Well you won't stop and I know you'll find it, halfway down the coast

You were never afraid of fighting, you blame an angry god
And when you see the first sign of violence, you bear it all as hard
When you held her son and wept I just felt jealous most of all
The best I had was near as bad as the sign of the rising fall

Though we're only alive a short while
So many beneath my feet
All weather you walk with me
And you were off on a wandering mile
I was holding a weak excuse
I was heavy beneath blue

---

*What does it mean to be immortal?*

1. Partially an ode to Victor Jara, folk musician and national hero in Chile, murdered
by henchmen of the dictator Pinochet. Victor and his memory live on in our collec-
tive memory and in his music; this song and the album as a whole are a celebration
of the immortality music can confer.

Now you're off to Victor on his ladder to the sky
And I'm left to sing it with you from my piece of the waterside
And you sang for the lost and gone who were young and deserving more
And now I'm stood upright all night ready when you come in the door

Though we're only alive a short while
So many beneath my feet
All weather you walk with me
And you were off on a wandering mile
I was holding a weak excuse
I was heavy beneath blue

All I heard
Wait for the word
You're coming with me

# FEATHERWEIGHT

SHORE / 03:50

# FEATHERWEIGHT[1]

All this time I've been hanging on
To an edge I caught when we both were young
That the world I want wasn't near enough
All was distant, always off

In all that war I'd forgotten how
Many men might die for what I'd renounce
I was staging life as a battleground
Now I let that grasping fall

May the last long year be forgiven
All that war left within it
I couldn't, though I'm beginning to
And we've only made it together

---

*Does the chorus always need to be the highest-sung part? Can a lower-sung chorus still be more ear-catching?*

1. This song tries to capture a greater sense of perspective than I was able to hold in my twenties, when my struggles and obligations seemed so big, and my options seemed so few. I'm ashamed I didn't enjoy that time more, and I hope to make the most of that sense in the future.

Feel some change in the weather
I couldn't though I'm beginning to

Though it's all so uncertain, cold
All the rafters cracked, all the copper sold
There's a ration back in a manifold
If you need it or forgot

May the last long year be forgiven
All that war left within it
I couldn't, though I'm beginning to
And we've only made it together
Feel some change in the weather
I couldn't though I'm beginning to

And somehow I see
It's free

And with love and hate in the balance
One last way past the malice
One warm day's all I really need
And with love and hate in the balance
One last way past the malice
One warm day is all I really need

# A LONG WAY
# PAST THE PAST
SHORE / 03:59

# A LONG WAY PAST THE PAST[1]

More than I had in mind
More than I wish I knew
And now it's near on me,
Some rush of red fear
And my worst old times look fine from here

I know you walked this route
And you might help me out
You said what's done is done
I can't turn the hand round
But still it looks a long way down

---

*Can this song tightrope-walk over the snake pit of corniness and survive?*

1. I've always loved old things: old music, old instruments, old furniture, old cars. Sometimes this nostalgic bent feels idealistic, enamored with a time when things were made with care and the world was simpler. Sometimes it feels nihilistic; a post-hoc justification for eras of history that were actually quite miserable socially for most people, with no hope for a better future. This song lives in the tension between these two senses. The first half is musically nostalgic and jovial, the second is vaguely futuristic and questioning. The question remains unresolved.

O man, was it that much better then?
We were left alone, we were proud of our pain
And so I want to walk out in the night
See the wide young river flood rain

We're not on one straight line
I made my own way through
And when the track goes cold
I'll know that it's true
That rebirth won't work like it used to

O man, was it that much better then?
We were left alone, we were proud of our pain
And so I want to walk out in the night
See the wide young river flood rain

And I can't let go
Of a lot I've left
I'm holding nothing
But what I kept
And it all got dimmer
Each passing step
And I need you with me
And you read the writ
Are you now insisting
Is it not worth it?
But I've got no option
I inherited this and I'm overcome

That's that, we're a long way from the past
I'll be better off in a year or in two

# FOR A WEEK
# OR TWO
SHORE / 02:11

# FOR A WEEK OR TWO[1]

Some lost coast
Some bright days
No face on your young head
Piece of wheat
In your teeth
Carrying water, pears and bread

And you're close to some surrender
You can feel it at your feet
And later on remember
When the fever broke and you could eat

And you've brought enough to last another week or two
Know the door is open, know that I miss you

---

*Can I make a few very short songs that feel like memories?*

1. More memories of time in nature written in the middle of lockdown, singing to a younger self, lost in a different wilderness.

You sought land
Overgrown
No words, no false, no true
Water stands
Waves just pass through it
Like something moves through you

# MAESTRANZA
SHORE / 03:03

# MAESTRANZA[1]

Monday night
Loud in the road outside
I saw the gate coming down
And smoke all around
The south hill
These last days
Con men controlled my fate
No one is holding the whip
And the oil won't stick
But I will

Now that a light is on
Now that the water runs
And the heartless are nearly gone
No time to get it wrong

---

*Can we build a rhythm track around multiple felted-piano parts treated with timed and panned delays?*

1. This song grew from the mid-pandemic paradox that, despite being physically and emotionally isolated, me and other members of my community were experiencing the exact same thing, alone together.

Sunday end
Ache for the sight of friends
Though I've been safe in the thought
That the line we walk
Is the same one

Now that a light is on
Now that the water runs
And the heartless are nearly gone
No time to get it wrong

Sometimes it comes to this, no it's true
This time, what comes of it, call it due
I do, I do, I do, I do

Now that a light is on
Now that the water runs
And the heartless are nearly gone
No time to get it wrong

# YOUNG MAN'S GAME
## SHORE / 03:11

# YOUNG MAN'S GAME[1]

New day rising, come close the blue blinds
I'll be lying in my ocean of time
I could dress as Arthur Lee[2]
Scrape my shoes the right way
Maybe read *Ulysses*[3]
But it's a young man's game

Dying fire, so tired of this place
Not inspired, can't keep to this pace
I could worry through each night
Find something unique to say
I could pass as erudite,
But it's a young man's game

---

*Can we let a song just be kind of dumb? Intentionally, this time, instead of unintentionally, like every other time?*

1. As I age, I feel really glad to be leaving the pretensions, postures, and anxieties of youth behind.

2. The singer of one of my favorite bands, Love, and one of my style icons as a teenager.

3. I've technically read this, but have I really?

You should know, you're my last hope

I've been solving for the meaning of life
No one tried before and likely I'm right
Not too straight or too clean
Like your borrowed blue bike
I've been a rolling antique
For all my life

You should know, you're my last hope

I've been lucky as sin
Not one thing in my way
Just the arena I was in
But it's a young man's game

# I'M NOT MY SEASON

SHORE / 03:11

# I'M NOT MY SEASON

Blood of my blood,
Skin of my skin,
You're in roundelay water again
I want to face the condition you're in
The old wrenches hardly turn me
Can you catch a thrown line?[1]
Tied around neat
Circle once about, please allow me
I see the pall coming off of our cheeks
We're weak but a leaf is turning

And I move lightly in the dawn
Try to, lightly ever on the lee

---

*Can we make a song that Nico might have covered?*

1. I took a sailing lesson once, and was struck by the very specific and codified system we were taught for rescuing someone who had fallen overboard. I related this to an experience a friend was then going through, trying to help a sibling of theirs through a struggle with opioid addiction.

Though I liked summer light on you
If we ride a winter-long wind
Well time's not what I belong to
And I'm not the season I'm in[2]

Holding on close
Holding on to
Any kind of ring I can bring you
And at the beach-wood pyre good news
It's wet but it's catching easy

And I move lightly in the dawn
Try to, gently ever on the lee

Though I liked summer light on you
If we ride a winter-long wind
Well time's not what I belong to
And you're not the season you're in

---

2. So much of songwriting hinges on finding new, defamiliarizing ways to express very familiar sentiments, in hopes of being able to reach ears that may be inoculated to true but tired clichés.

# QUIET AIR / GIOIA

SHORE / 04:27

# QUIET AIR / GIOIA[1]

Quiet air, quiet in blue
Quiet ice melt, summer-red cedar
Quiet air might terrify you
Quiet now though soon enough louder
Some shape, float on faith in the eye

You want to go where the fire is worst
You want to watch our tower drop to the water
I know you don't want anyone else hurt
I know you don't, you're better, you're stronger
Some shape, float on faith in the eye
Some shape, floating in the eye

---

*How many layers of counterpoint can we fit in a house song?*

1. One sinister reality of our current climate crisis is the creeping silence of carbon dioxide accruing in the air; the sense that something is quietly and invisibly amassing, causing irreparable harm to our environment; a sense of being frogs, slowly boiling, not noticing before it's too late.

I'll be alone in the corduroy heath
I'll wait a long time till the hard rain is over
You're alone and you're calling on me
I'm underneath my canopy colder
Some shape, float on faith in the eye
Some shape, floating in the eye

Feeling a gold unfolding hand on me
Nowhere to go, no one I'd rather see
Oh devil walk by, oh devil walk by
I never want to die, I never want to die

# GOING-TO-THE-
# SUN ROAD
SHORE / 03:58

# GOING-TO-THE-SUN ROAD[1]

Due west at a blind day's end, flying pavement underfoot
Some horizon eyeing me up, often does right at dusk
Often known it wore that look

And I've known it one too many times
And the thought of flight for water whiter
Now those passing dotted lines
Going on and on just shake my sleep all night
Could be I'm finally losing my fight

Due south all the fog aired out, no idea where all this leads
Though I still wanted to show Going-to-the-Sun Road to you,
Still got one in me

---

*Can I capture what I think a place sounds like, even if I've never been there?*

1. Yet another place I've never been, the beautiful Going-to-the-Sun Road in Glacier
National Park, Montana. I've been holding this in my mind as the greatest possible
American road trip, but I've been hesitant to actually go. I've been saving it for some
special moment, but maybe it's better to just leave it as an unfulfilled curiosity.

If I want to, I'll arrive at peace
I know I decide what I remember
If this ever mended me
All the on and on
Just shakes my sleep all night
Now I'm losing my fight

A estrada do sol
O começo de tudo
E as nuvens que agora se afastam
Mostrando um caminho que está sempre lá
E que é qualquer lado que a gente quiser caminhar

# THYMIA
SHORE / 02:22

# THYMIA[1]

Pair of tin cups rolling in the back seat
Rustle like a mallet on a downbeat
Rain will make rust, water on the concrete

Have a true love, more than just an outline
Solid shape of, known it for a long time
Never failed us, even losing daylight
Daylight

Thymia, accompany us
All the way to Townsend

---

*How many chords can I fit under one simple melody? Can I make a B section of song just from changing the chords, and make the melody feel different, even though it's re-maining static?*

1. For a couple of years in my mid-twenties, while making *Helplessness Blues*, I lived in Port Townsend, Washington, a faded Victorian maritime village on the Quimper Peninsula. I would regularly make long drives into Seattle, to gather recording equipment or to see friends and family. On one of those drives, some loose camping equipment in the back seat was clanking out a musical beat against some regular bumps in the pavement, and I remember singing along, with a sense that music for me was somehow inescapable—would always be, for better and worse. This song is an evocation of that memory.

How to explain, moving as a phantom?
Falling like rain, over and abandoned

Thymia, accompany us
All the way to Townsend

# CRADLING MOTHER,
# CRADLING WOMAN
SHORE / 05:10

# CRADLING MOTHER, CRADLING WOMAN[1]

I'll run down
Lay my weight where it lies
I'll come round
Out in sheltering sky
Seek you out
Like I wanted it when
It was eighty-eight out
And the apricot flowers were coming in

And I feel worn, but the air is clean
And my clothes are torn, but it's right on me
Passing rain, blue-white heat
Agony, not to me, it's not defeat

---

*What if all the music at once?*

1. This title comes from a mistranslation into English of "Ama Dablam," the name of a mountain in the Himalayas, in northeastern Nepal. I took a monthlong hiking trip in that region, alone, when I was twenty-seven. I was feeling lost and full of wanderlust in equal measure, but as beautiful as the scenery was, I regretted going by myself. Along the trail, there was this distinctive mountain. It seemed to be peeking around every corner, every day, at every step along the way. I eventually asked someone on the road what it was called and he said—"that's Ama Dablam—cradling mother, or cradling woman." The name really translates as "mother's necklace," I believe, but I came out of the trip with a song title, and the resolve to never again undertake such an adventure alone.

No one here
Say we waited our while
Good idea
Crowding out of those aisles
Nowhere near
Where I thought we would be
But one and the same
The drought and the rain to me

And I've been a while gone
But the air is clean
And I had it all wrong
But I made my peace
Passing thought, empty street
Agony, not to me, it's not defeat

I've been bright, I've been faded
I'm nearly halfway through
Barely believe we made it
When I met eyes with you
I caught a walking fever
I know how all this ends
Palm over my receiver
Cradling me again

# SHORE

SHORE / 04:19

# SHORE

Kin of my kin, I rely on you
Taking me in, when a wave runs me through
As a shore I ever seem to sail to
And I know old heavinesses shake you

Maybe I stayed little long, could be
I needed shade, sand on my feet
And it's some new ailment is in me
Can't divide what's memory and what's dream

Afraid of the empty, but too safe on the shore
And 'fore I forget me
I want to record[1]

While I see it all
While I see it all

---

*What does relief sound like? What does a cliffhanger sound like?*

1. Recording music as an act of preserving memory.

I remember[2] walking shoulders hours speaking
I remember meeting Clementine[3] and weeping
I remember Prine,[4] I remember you
After word of Berman I remember Pfeiffer burning[5]
I remember hoping I'd remember nothing
Now I only hope I'm holding onto something

Now the quarter moon[6] is out
Now the quarter moon is out[7]

---

2. Anaphora inspired by Joe Brainard's seminal memoir *I Remember*.

3. My niece.

4. John Prine, may he rest in peace.

5. I was in Big Sur for the Soberanes fire in 2016.

6. The release of this album was timed for an equinox that also happened to fall on a quarter moon.

7. Thank you for reading :)

# AFTERWORD
Robin Pecknold

Growing up, I loved the most basic, antipoetic lyrics. Lyrics about wanting to hold hands, how the times are changing, being a jealous man, being very sad sometimes, being in love with a girl. My teenage mind marveled not at the words themselves, but at how impactful they became when paired with inventive instrumentation and canny melodies, how layers of meaning and identification would alchemize when a lyric collided with arrangement, timbre, delivery, tempo, key, and meter. I liked phonemic choices and elisions that seemed butter smooth, sanded to a finish. I liked judicious use of internal rhyme, alliteration, and anaphora. I liked lyrics that were emotionally rich but technically invisible, no hanging syllables or Germanic consonants, like paintings that hide their brushstrokes. I liked lyrics that weren't trying to sell a false promise or an easy answer. And above all, I liked coherent, sturdy, undeniable melodies, the metric ton of horsepower a good melody could infuse into any well-set lyric. Now, at thirty-six, past retirement age in Rock Years, I still feel the same. I'm not sure if we really change as we get older. Maybe we just get confused for a while by something or other, and eventually circle back to wherever it was we unselfconsciously began—a bit wiser, a few more questions answered.

I'm honored that Tin House has published these words, but I'm also a bit embarrassed, because I don't really identify as a lyricist, or even as a writer. I do make time most every day to sit down, sing into a microphone, and seek out song ideas, but I never sit down to write lyrics. I only ever "write" words while actively singing; the lyrics always start as a confused cloud of vocalese gibberish. Over the course of hours of searching repetition, this gibberish congeals around one or two repeated sounds, utterances that braid well with melodies I'm simultaneously trying to find. Those sounds inevitably suggest a handful of possible phrases; those phrases suggest concepts; those concepts suggest elaborations and refutations. It goes on like this, order arising from chaos, until there's a finished lyric that reveals some emotional truth I didn't at first intend to share, and often don't consciously understand. Maybe this is how the process works for real writers, too, but it never feels like writing to me. It feels more like discovering something.

If a bottle of water in a freezer is clean enough, the water will remain liquid; to initiate the freezing process, ice crystals need a speck of dust or other impurity to attach to. Similarly, in finding lyrics, there's usually one word or phrase that floats in, sticks, and catalyzes a chain reaction. I remember sitting in the dark in our old Seattle recording space, the same dingy triangular room where Nirvana made *Bleach*, singing and playing into a broken PA, writing the song "Helplessness Blues." I was repeating a strummed chord, finding that trancelike space where my songs come from, tracing the jutting arc of the melody and singing "something something believing . . ." over and over. The rest of the lyrics arose out of the implications present in that word "believing," a word that itself arose randomly in the process of finding the melody. And in the years since, whenever people have shown me the lyrics to "Helplessness Blues" tattooed on their skin, I always think back to those gloaming hours singing nascent gibberish in the dark;

it's a marvel that lyrics born so randomly could come to live permanently on a forearm or a clavicle.

Or in a book! Compiling and notating the lyrics here was maybe the first time I'd read them together, and one thing I kept noticing was the preponderance of question marks. I counted eighty-eight in total, about two per song, and one per key on the average piano. This reminded me of how fundamental the asking of questions has always been to my songwriting—not just with words, but with the music itself. Creatively, I'm most excited when the song I'm working on seems to be posing an interesting question, when it embodies some combination of elements or conceits that hasn't been attempted in exactly that way before. A question could be micro or macro; it could be teasing out unexplored implications of other beloved music; it could be strictly lyrical, strictly musical, or both. To me, a song is "good" if it is asking interesting questions. And a song is "done" when those questions are no longer confusing the song's maker.

Can I fit two choruses into a four-minute song? What if the Beach Boys were Trappist monks? What does the Pacific Northwest, as I've experienced it, sound like? Can I blend six genres at once? How did the greats used to record? How might people be recording in five years? Can I be so emotionally vulnerable that it's uncomfortable? How many chords can gracefully support this one melody? Can I get away with saving the best part of this song for minute three? Minute five? Can an eight-minute-long song hold one's attention? How much can happen in two minutes? What's a guitar tuning no one else has ever used? Can a song start as a sentence that's describing imaginary music? What if a song's structure resembled nonlinear film editing? How many octaves can I sing across in one song? Can listening to a song feel like being trapped on a sinking ship? Can it feel like Elysium?

Seeking answers to questions like these is what compelled me to make songs in the first place. Sometimes I'll just make long lists of questions, all songs yet to be made, and I'll spend afternoons and evenings teasing out answers to each one. If a question goes nowhere, so be it, but I find it impossible to separate curiosity from creativity. As I get older, I find it harder to come up with new questions that are not only compelling, but that I haven't tried to answer at least once before, and so I write fewer songs. But I much prefer that songwriting lives in the space of "seeing what he could see," even if it's just the other side of the mountain, than in the space of having everything, or anything, figured out. It's much more fulfilling to me to seek new questions than to rely on old answers.

The most recent musical question I found myself asking while making an album was "What if I could write only one more song? What would I want that to be?" It was the peak of summer 2020, and I had nowhere to go in the world but out for a drive, aimlessly away from our then-dim present. I had one lyric left to finish for the album *Shore*, a stubborn song called "Sunblind." I wanted the song to function as a statement of intent for the whole record, but it remained unfinished. Studios were closed and I had nowhere to work, so I was in the habit of driving nowhere in particular down country roads for eight or ten hours a day, feeling the warm breeze through the open windows, listening to David Berman, Judee Sill, Elliott Smith, Richard Swift, John Prine, Bill Withers, Arthur Russell, Duncan Browne, Joy Division, Tim Buckley, Chris Bell, Jimi Hendrix, Nick Drake, Otis Redding, and Marvin Gaye: all lost heroes who left us too soon. I was trying, in that grim season, to honor loss by reacquainting myself with this music that had meant so much to me over the years, these people whose loss I still feel.

On one of my drives, I got turned around looking for a swimming hole, and instead ended up winding down desolate, boarded-up Main Streets, past graveyards and pop-up COVID testing centers and empty baseball fields. Seeing all this, with my playlist of lost heroes on the stereo, it struck me that maybe I should write "The Last Fleet Foxes Song," just in case, because who knows, or rather who knew anything, in the summer of 2020. I realized that if I could write only one last song, I'd want it to be an elegy to, and a commemoration of, other musicians, in that delicate tradition of songs about music itself, like David Berman's "Snow Is Falling in Manhattan" or ABBA's "Thank You for the Music." I don't think I'd have any last words of my own; most of the questions I've posed in my lyrics remain unresolved for me anyway. What's there to really say at the end of it all except "thank you"?

I appreciate now having a place in a chain. "Sunblind" stands squarely between the older musicians I'm honoring and the younger musicians who may be listening in for the first time. In that spirit, and on the off chance that "Sunblind" actually is the last Fleet Foxes song and no second volume of lyrics will come out in ten years, I want to offer some brief, more explicit parting words of advice to any young songwriters who might be reading this.

It's okay to be insecure; in many ways insecurity works to your benefit. Anyone too pleased with what they're doing is either delusional or not aiming high enough. Think about songs as questions to be answered; it helps to depersonalize an already fraught process. If you want to get rid of writer's block, get rid of any concept of a writer; think about songs as things you're finding more than things you're making. You always have permission to do whatever you want creatively, regardless of how true that might feel in the moment. Be as courteous with your listener as you would be with a respected guest in your home. It's up to you to set their expectations, and also to endeavor to exceed them—take advantage of that aspect of having their attention. All good art has some quality of defamiliarization to it, some sense of novelty, some combination of elements that seem to present an alternate view of reality. The first line of a song colors the listener's perception of everything after it. Every great album has at least four undeniably good songs on it and no less—focus on those four first. Work with people you feel safe around and avoid narcissists. Some degree of certainty is necessary, but it's always temporary. Know when to freeze and when to melt. If you want to end up with ten great songs, try to find, say, fifty ideas with potential; arrive at quality via quantity. Don't be afraid to throw things out, or cobble songs together from the very best bits of everything you've tried. Don't go back to school at age twenty-six and abandon your career at its peak, and don't take anything that other artists are doing too personally. Life is too damn short and music is too damn sacred.

Thank you to Brandon Taylor, Masie Cochran, and Craig Popelars at Tin House, Aja Pecknold, Sean Pecknold, Lisa Pecknold, and Greg Pecknold. Thank you to Joanna Newsom, my musical and lyrical hero. And thank you to everyone who has supported the music of Fleet Foxes over the years. You have been incredibly generous and we have been unspeakably lucky.